Waiting for Christ's Return

Studies on Hope

Based on *When Christ Comes*

Max Lucado

General Editor

Contents

Introduction

So many joys await us on the day of Christ's return!

A day of reunion, a day of rewards, a day of redemption. For Satan, it will be the end of evil. But for God's children, it will be the beginning of everlasting celebration.

Knowing this, then, how will we live? Should we live in fear of the return? Or should we live joyfully, expectantly? God wants us to trust him: "Don't let your hearts be troubled. Trust in God, and trust in me....I will come back and take you to be with me" (Jn. 14:1, 3). Setting our hearts on heaven, leaving the details to the Father, let's study together the day when Christ comes—the beginning of the very best.

—*Max Lucado*

Day of Fulfilled Expectations

"Thoughts of the Second Coming unsettle me. Life with no end? Space with no bounds? And what about Armageddon, the lake of fire, the mark of the beast? Am I supposed to understand all this? Am I supposed to feel good about all this?" —Max Lucado

1

1. Think about everything you've heard about Christ's coming and the end of the world as we know it. What parts leave you feeling the most unsettled?

_____

_____

_____

_____

_____

_____

_____

A Moment with Max

Max shares these insights with us in his book *When Christ Comes*.

What is the single query hated most by moms and dads? It's the one posed by the five-year-old on the trip, "How much farther?"

Give us the dilemmas of geometry and sexuality, just don't make a parent answer the question, "How much farther?"

It's an impossible question. How do you speak of time and distance to someone who doesn't understand time and distance? The world of a youngster is delightfully free of mile-markers and alarm clocks. You can speak of minutes and kilometers, but a child has no hooks for those hats.

Sooner or later, they ask again. And sooner or later, we say what all parents eventually say, "Just trust me. You enjoy the trip and don't worry about the details. I'll make sure we get home OK."

And we mean it. We don't want our kids to sweat the details. So we make a deal with them, "We'll do the taking. You do the trusting."

Sound familiar? It might. Jesus has said the same to us. Just prior to his crucifixion, he told his disciples that he would be leaving them. (John 13:36).

2. How is waiting for Christ's return a lot like being a child on a long trip?

2

_____

_____

_____

_____

_____

_____

3. What's so difficult about facing the unknown?

_____

_____

_____

_____

_____

A Message from the Word

33Jesus said, "My children, I will be with you only a little longer. You will look for me, and what I told the Jews, I tell you now: Where I am going you cannot come.

34"I give you a new command: Love each other. You must love each other as I have loved you. 35All people will know that you are my followers if you love each other."

36Simon Peter asked Jesus, "Lord, where are you going?"

Jesus answered, "Where I am going you cannot follow now, but you will follow later."

37Peter asked, "Lord, why can't I follow you now? I am ready to die for you!"

38Jesus answered, "Are you ready to die for me? I tell you the truth, before the rooster crows, you will say three times that you don't know me."

1Jesus said, "Don't let your hearts be troubled. Trust in God, and trust in me. 2There are many rooms in my Father's house; I would not tell you this if it were not true. I am going there to prepare a place for you. 3After I go and prepare a place for you, I will come back and take you to be with me so that you may be where I am. 4You know the way to the place where I am going."

5Thomas said to Jesus, "Lord, we don't know where you are going. So how can we know the way?"

6Jesus answered, "I am the way, and the truth, and the life. The only way to the Father is through me. 7If you really knew me, you would know my Father, too. But now you do know him, and you have seen him."

John 13:33-14:7

4. Describe what the disciples must have felt when they heard Jesus say he was leaving them?

_____

_____

_____

_____

_____

3

5. What kind of questions would you have wanted to ask Jesus in the course of this conversation?

_____

_____

_____

_____

_____

6. From what you know about Jesus' death and resurrection, what do you think he was preparing the disciples to do?

_____

_____

4 _____

_____

_____

_____

More From The Word

²³Jesus answered, "If people love me, they will obey my teaching. My Father will love them, and we will come to them and make our home with them. ²⁴Those who do not love me do not obey my teaching. This teaching that you hear is not really mine; it is from my Father, who sent me.

²⁵"I have told you all these things while I am with you. ²⁶But the Helper will teach you everything and will cause you to remember all that I told you. This Helper is the Holy Spirit whom the Father will send in my name.

²⁷"I leave you peace; my peace I give you. I do not give it to you as the

world does. So don't let your hearts be troubled or afraid. [28]You heard me say to you, 'I am going, but I am coming back to you.' If you loved me, you should be happy that I am going back to the Father, because he is greater than I am. [29]I have told you this now, before it happens, so that when it happens, you will believe."

John 14:23-29

7. How do Jesus' words to his disciples encourage us in our wait for his second coming?

_____

_____

_____

_____

_____

8. What role does the Holy Spirit play in our lives as we prepare for Christ's return?

5

_____

_____

_____

_____

9. What similarities can you draw between the trust the disciples needed to have in Christ's words and the trust we need to have in them?

_____

_____

_____

_____

_____

My Reflections

"All of his words can be reduced to two: *Trust me.* Don't be troubled by the return of Christ. Don't be anxious about things you cannot comprehend. Issues like the millennium and the Antichrist are intended to challenge and stretch us, but not overwhelm and certainly not divide us. For the Christian, the return of Christ is not a riddle to be solved or a code to be broken, but rather a day to be anticipated. He knows exactly what you need. You needn't worry about getting bored or tired or weary with seeing the same people or singing the same songs. He is preparing the perfect place for you." —Max

Journal

6

How can I trust God with my concerns about the future?

_____

_____

_____

_____

_____

_____

_____

_____

_____

_____

_____

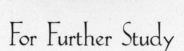

For Further Study

To study more about trusting God when facing the unknown, read Psalm 37:35-40; Proverbs 23:18-25; Isaiah 41:10; Matthew 26:64; Romans 8:37-39; 1 Peter 3:13-17.

Additional Questions

10. What concerns do you have about the future?

_____

_____

_____

_____

_____

_____

11. How is it comforting to know that God knows every detail of your future?

_____

_____

_____

_____

_____

_____

12. What do you look forward to most about your future in heaven?

_____

_____

_____

_____

_____

_____

Additional Thoughts

_____

_____

9

_____

_____

_____

_____

_____

_____

_____

_____

_____

_____

_____

10

Day to Anticipate

"*Some Christians are so obsessed with the last days that they are oblivious to these days. Others are just the opposite. They'll tell you Jesus is coming. But they live like he never will. One is too panicky, the other too patient. Isn't there a balance?*" —*Max Lucado*

11

1. What kinds of things have you heard people say they hope they can do before they die or Jesus returns?

_____

_____

_____

_____

_____

_____

_____

A Moment with Max

Max shares these insights with us in his book *When Christ Comes.*

What does it do to you if you know you will someday see God? We know what it did to Simeon.

He was "constantly expecting the Messiah" (Luke 2:25 TLB).

Maybe you know what it's like to look for someone who has come for you. I do. When I travel somewhere to speak, I often don't know who will pick me up at the airport. Someone has been sent, but I don't know the person. Hence, I exit the plane searching the faces for a face I've never seen. But though I've never seen the person, I know I'll find him.

I bet Simeon would have said the same. Studying each passing face. Staring into the eyes of strangers. He's looking for someone.

He was waiting *forwardly.* Patiently vigilant. Calmly expectant. Eyes open. Arms extended. Searching the crowd for the right face, and hoping the face appears today.

2. What feelings or thoughts come to mind when you think of waiting for someone?

12 _____

_____

_____

_____

_____

3. How would you describe the balance between waiting for Christ's return and investing in this life?

_____

_____

_____

_____

_____

A Message from the Word

²⁵In Jerusalem lived a man named Simeon who was a good man and godly. He was waiting for the time when God would take away Israel's sorrow, and the Holy Spirit was in him. ²⁶Simeon had been told by the Holy Spirit that he would not die before he saw the Christ promised by the Lord. ²⁷The Spirit led Simeon to the Temple. When Mary and Joseph brought the baby Jesus to the Temple to do what the law said they must do, ²⁸Simeon took the baby in his arms and thanked God:

²⁹"Now, Lord, you can let me, your servant,
    die in peace as you said.
³⁰With my own eyes I have seen your salvation,
    ³¹which you prepared before all people.
³²It is a light for the non-Jewish people to see
    and an honor for your people, the Israelites."

³³Jesus' father and mother were amazed at what Simeon had said about him. ³⁴Then Simeon blessed them and said to Mary, "God has chosen this child to cause the fall and rise of many in Israel. He will be a sign from God that many people will not accept ³⁵so that the thoughts of many will be made known. And the things that will happen will make your heart sad, too."

Luke 2:25-35

4. After all that Mary and Joseph had experienced during her pregnancy and Christ's birth, why do you think they marveled at Simeon's words?

_____

_____

_____

_____

5. How would you feel as a parent if you had received Simeon's blessing?

_____

_____

_____

_____

6. How is Simeon's example a model for how we should await Jesus' second coming?

_____

_____

_____

_____

More From The Word

[10]But the day of the Lord will come like a thief. The skies will disappear with a loud noise. Everything in them will be destroyed by fire, and the earth and everything in it will be burned up. [11]In that way everything will be destroyed. So what kind of people should you be? You should live holy lives and serve God, [12]as you wait for and look forward to the coming of the day of God. When that day comes, the skies will be destroyed with fire, and everything in them will melt with heat. [13]But God made a promise to us, and we are waiting for a new heaven and a new earth where goodness lives.

[14]Dear friends, since you are waiting for this to happen, do your best to be without sin and without fault. Try to be at peace with God.

2 Peter 3:10-14

7. How does this description of how we should live compare with the description of how Simeon lived in the hope of Christ's arrival?

_____

_____

_____

_____

_____

8. Describe someone you know who truly lives looking forward to Christ's return.

_____

_____

_____

_____

_____

9. List some reasons why our hope of Christ's return prompts us to live holy lives.

_____

_____

_____

_____

_____

My Reflections

"Haven't we, like Simeon been told of the coming Christ? Aren't we, like Simeon, heirs of a promise? Are we not prompted by the same Spirit? Are we not longing to see the same face? Simeon reminds us to 'wait forwardly.' Patiently vigilant. But not so patient that we lose our vigilance. Nor so vigilant that we lose our patience. One look into the face of Jesus, and Simeon knew it was time to go home. And one look into the face of our Savior, and we will know the same." —Max

Journal

How can I strike a better balance between patience and vigilance in waiting for Christ's return?

_____

_____

_____

_____

_____

_____

_____

_____

_____

_____

_____

_____

_____

_____

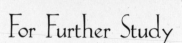

For Further Study

To study more about believing God's promises, read Psalm 119:49-56; Psalm 119:75-82; Psalm 145:13-16; Romans 4:18-22; Hebrews 12:22-27; 2 Peter 3:8-13; 1 John 2:24-25.

Additional Questions

10. What do you think causes some people to become obsessed with the end of the world?

_____

_____

_____

_____

_____

11. How do you think Simeon knew Jesus was the Messiah?

_____

_____

_____

_____

_____

12. What things stand in the way of people recognizing and believing Jesus is the Messiah?

_____

_____

_____

_____

_____

_____

_____

Additional Thoughts

_____

_____

_____

_____

_____

_____

_____

_____

_____

_____

_____

Day of Proof and Preview

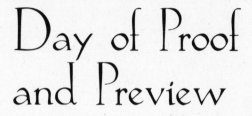

*"**I**'m the cautious type. I want to believe in Jesus' promise to return, but can I? Dare I trust the words of a small-town carpenter spoken two thousand years ago in a remote nation? Can I really believe in what Jesus says about his coming?"* —Max Lucado

21

1. What do you think is the most difficult thing about Jesus for most people to believe?

_____

_____

_____

_____

_____

_____

_____

A Moment with Max

Max shares these insights with us in his book *When Christ Comes*.

Christ's death was real. For three days Jesus' body decayed. It did not rest, mind you. It decayed. The cheeks sank and the skin paled. But after three days the process was reversed. There was a stirring, a stirring deep within the grave...and the living Christ stepped forth.

And the moment he stepped forth, everything changed. As Paul stated: "When Jesus was raised from the dead it was a signal of the end of death-as-the-end" (Romans 6:5–6 MSG).

Because we can accept the resurrection story, it is safe to accept the rest of the story. Because of the resurrection, everything changes.

Death changes. It used to be the end; now it is the beginning.

The cemetery changes. People once went there to say good-bye; now they go to say, "We'll be together again."

And someday according to Christ, he will set us free. He will come back. And to prove that he was serious about his promise, the stone was rolled and his body was raised.

Someday in the blink of an eye, as fast as the lightning flashes from the east to the west, he will come back. And everyone will see him—you will, I will. Bodies will push back the dirt and break the surface of the sea. The earth will tremble, the sky will roar, and those who do not know him will shudder. But in that hour you will not fear, because you know him.

2. What words do you think best describe what Christ's resurrection was like for the people who were actually living at the time?

_____

_____

_____

_____

3. How does Christ's resurrection change your view of death?

_____

_____

_____

_____

A Message from the Word

¹The day after the Sabbath day was the first day of the week. At dawn on the first day, Mary Magdalene and another woman named Mary went to look at the tomb.

²At that time there was a strong earthquake. An angel of the Lord came down from heaven, went to the tomb, and rolled the stone away from the entrance. Then he sat on the stone. ³He was shining as bright as lightning, and his clothes were white as snow. ⁴The soldiers guarding the tomb shook with fear because of the angel, and they became like dead men.

⁵The angel said to the women, "Don't be afraid. I know that you are looking for Jesus, who has been crucified. ⁶He is not here. He has risen from the dead as he said he would. Come and see the place where his body was. ⁷And go quickly and tell his followers, 'Jesus has risen from the dead. He is going into Galilee ahead of you, and you will see him there.' "Then the angel said, "Now I have told you."

⁸The women left the tomb quickly. They were afraid, but they were also very happy. They ran to tell Jesus' followers what had happened. ⁹Suddenly, Jesus met them and said, "Greetings." The women came up to him, took hold of his feet, and worshiped him. ¹⁰Then Jesus said to them, "Don't be afraid. Go and tell my followers to go on to Galilee, and they will see me there."

¹¹While the women went to tell Jesus' followers, some of the soldiers who had been guarding the tomb went into the city to tell the leading priests everything that had happened. ¹²Then the priests met with the older Jewish leaders and made a plan. They paid the soldiers a large amount of money ¹³and said to them, "Tell the people that Jesus' followers came during the night and stole the body while you were asleep. ¹⁴If the governor hears about this, we will satisfy him and save you from trouble." ¹⁵So the soldiers kept the money and did as they were told. And that story is still spread among the Jewish people even today.

Matthew 28:1-15

4. Describe what Christ's resurrection must have meant to those women who had followed him and supported his ministry.

_____

_____

_____

5. Describe what Christ's resurrection must have meant to the disciples who had pledged their allegiance and accepted the responsibility to carry on his work.

_____

_____

_____

_____

_____

6. What does Christ's resurrection mean for us, specifically as we look forward to his return?

_____

_____

_____

_____

_____

More From The Word

[1]So do you think we should continue sinning so that God will give us even more grace?[2]No! We died to our old sinful lives, so how can we continue living with sin?[3]Did you forget that all of us became part of Christ when we were baptized? We shared his death in our baptism. [4]When we were baptized, we were buried with Christ and shared his death. So, just as Christ was raised from the dead by the wonderful power of the Father, we also can live a new life.

[5]Christ died, and we have been joined with him by dying too. So we will also be joined with him by rising from the dead as he did. [6]We know that our old life died with Christ on the cross so that our sinful selves would have no power over us and we would not be slaves to sin. [7]Anyone who has died is made free from sin's control.

[8]If we died with Christ, we know we will also live with him. [9]Christ was raised from the dead, and we know that he cannot die again. Death has no power over him now. [10]Yes, when Christ died, he died to defeat the power of sin one time—enough for all time. He now has a new life, and his new life is with God.

Romans 6:1-10

7. Why do you believe that Jesus was raised from the dead?

_____

_____

_____

_____

8. What comfort is there in knowing that life extends beyond the grave?

_____

_____

_____

_____

9. Would you live your life differently if death meant your soul merely disappeared?

_____

_____

_____

_____

My Reflections

"The promise is simply this: The resurrection of Jesus is proof and preview of our own. But can we trust the promise? Is the resurrection a reality? Are the claims of the empty tomb true? This is not only a good question. It is *the* question. For as Paul wrote, 'If Christ has not been raised, then your faith has nothing to it; you are still guilty of your sins' (1 Corinthians 15:17). In other words, if Christ has been raised, then his followers will join him; but if not, then his followers are fools. You have heard the promise of your Father. You know that he has moved the stone. And in the moment he removed the stone, he also removed all reason for doubt. We can believe the words of our Father: 'I will come back and take you to be with me so that you may be where I am' (John 14:3)." —Max

Journal

How can I strengthen my beliefs in God's promises?

_____

_____

_____

_____

_____

_____

_____

_____

For Further Study

To study more about the resurrection from the dead, read Matthew 27:50-53; John 11:11-44; Acts 24:10-21; Philippians 3:10-11; 1 Peter 1:3-5; Revelation 20:4-6.

Additional Questions

10. In what ways do you think Christ's resurrection was difficult to believe at the time it happened?

_____

_____

_____

_____

_____

_____

11. In what different ways is the resurrection difficult to believe today?

_____

_____

_____

_____

_____

_____

12. Which do you think is more difficult to believe: that Jesus rose from the dead or that he is coming back again for us?

_____

_____

_____

_____

_____

_____

Additional Thoughts

_____

_____

_____

_____

_____

_____

_____

_____

_____

_____

Day of Glad Reunions

"What about my loved ones who have died? Where are they now? In the time between our death and Christ's return, what happens?"

—Max Lucado

31

1. Describe someone you are really looking forward to seeing when you get to heaven.

_____

_____

_____

_____

_____

_____

_____

A Moment with Max

Max shares these insights with us in his book *When Christ Comes.*

We don't like to say good-bye to those we love.

But we have to. Try as we might to avoid it, as reluctant as we are to discuss it, death is a very real part of life. Each one of us must release the hand of one we love into the hand of one we have not seen.

Scripture is surprisingly quiet about this phase of our lives. When speaking about the period between the death of the body and the resurrection of the body, the Bible doesn't shout; it just whispers. But at the confluence of these whispers, a firm voice is heard. This authoritative voice assures us that, at death, the Christian immediately enters into the presence of God and enjoys conscious fellowship with the Father and with those who have gone before.

Where do I get such ideas?

I desire to depart and be with Christ, which is better by far. (Philippians 1:23 NIV)

The language here suggests an immediate departure of the soul after death.

Isn't this the promise that Jesus gave the thief on the cross? "I tell you the truth, today you will be with me in paradise" (Luke 23:43).

2. Describe the experience of someone who has been with a dying person when they passed from this life to the next.

_____

_____

_____

_____

3. What do you imagine you will experience when you take your last breath here on earth?

_____

_____

_____

_____

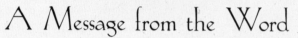

A Message from the Word

¹³Brothers and sisters, we want you to know about those Christians who have died so you will not be sad, as others who have no hope. ¹⁴We believe that Jesus died and that he rose again. So, because of him, God will raise with Jesus those who have died. ¹⁵What we tell you now is the Lord's own message. We who are living when the Lord comes again will not go before those who have already died. ¹⁶The Lord himself will come down from heaven with a loud command, with the voice of the archangel, and with the trumpet call of God. And those who have died believing in Christ will rise first. ¹⁷After that, we who are still alive will be gathered up with them in the clouds to meet the Lord in the air. And we will be with the Lord forever. ¹⁸So encourage each other with these words.

¹Now, brothers and sisters, we do not need to write you about times and dates. ²You know very well that the day the Lord comes again will be a surprise, like a thief that comes in the night. ³While people are saying, "We have peace and we are safe," they will be destroyed quickly. It is like pains that come quickly to a woman having a baby. Those people will not escape.

1 Thessalonians 4:13—5:3

4. How do you respond to the fact that when Jesus comes back for you he'll bring with him the Christians you have lost through death?

_____

_____

_____

_____

5. Why do you think God will gather the dead first?

_____

_____

_____

_____

6. How do you think family relationships will work in the afterlife?

_____

_____

_____

_____

_____

More From The Word

[23]That same day some Sadducees came to Jesus and asked him a question. (Sadducees believed that people would not rise from the dead.)[24]They said, "Teacher, Moses said if a married man dies without having children, his brother must marry the widow and have children for him. [25]Once there were seven brothers among us. The first one married and died. Since he had no children, his brother married the widow. [26]Then the second brother also died. The same thing happened to the third brother and all the other brothers. [27]Finally, the woman died. [28]Since all seven men had married her, when people rise from the dead, whose wife will she be?"

[29]Jesus answered, "You don't understand, because you don't know what the Scriptures say, and you don't know about the power of God. [30]When people rise from the dead, they will not marry, nor will they be given to someone to marry. They will be like the angels in heaven. [31]Surely you have read what God said to you about rising from the dead. [32]God said, 'I am the God of Abraham, the God of Isaac, and the God of Jacob.' God is the God of the living, not the dead."

Matthew 22:23-32

7. How do you feel about the fact that earthly marriages won't have the same meaning in heaven as they do on earth?

_____

_____

_____

_____

8. What other relationships, besides marriages, do you think will be different in heaven?

_____

_____

_____

_____

_____

9. How does the promise of seeing our deceased loved ones again affect our grieving for them?

_____

_____

_____

_____

_____

My Reflections

"If you'll celebrate a marriage anniversary alone this year, he speaks to you. If your child made it to heaven before making it to kindergarten, he speaks to you. If you lost a loved one in violence, if you learned more than you want to know about disease, if your dreams were buried as they lowered the casket, God speaks to you. He speaks to all of us who have stood or will stand in the soft dirt near an open grave. God transforms our hopeless grief into hope-filled grief. How? By telling us that we will see our loved ones again." —Max

Journal

What grief in my life does God want to turn into joy?

For Further Study

To study more about life after death, read Psalm 16:9–11; Daniel 12:1–3; Matthew 19:29; Matthew 25:31–46; Luke 16:19–31; John 3:12–16; John 6:45–47; 1 Timothy 6:12.

Additional Questions

10. Why is it so difficult to say good-bye to those we love, even knowing we'll be reunited one day in heaven?

_____

_____

_____

_____

_____

11. What comfort did someone give you at a time of loss? How can you do the same?

_____

_____

_____

_____

_____

12. What are you most looking forward to about heaven?

_____

_____

_____

_____

_____

Additional Thoughts

_____

_____

_____

_____

_____

_____

_____

_____

_____

_____

_____

40

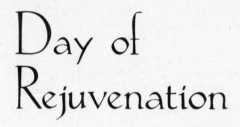

Day of Rejuvenation

"What's all this talk about a new body? Do we change bodies? Is the new one different than this one? Will I recognize anyone? Will anyone recognize me?" —Max Lucado

41

1. If you had the power to make the decision, what would you change about the human body in heaven?

_____

_____

_____

_____

_____

_____

_____

A Moment with Max

Max shares these insights with us in his book *When Christ Comes*.

Would you like a sneak preview of your new body? We have one by looking at the resurrected body of our Lord. After his resurrection, Jesus spent forty days in the presence of people. The resurrected Christ was not in a disembodied, purely spiritual state. On the contrary, he had a body—a touchable, visible body.

Jesus didn't come as a mist or a wind or a ghostly specter. He came in a body. A body that maintained a substantial connection with the body he originally had. A body that had flesh and bones. For did he not tell his followers, "A spirit has not flesh and bones as you see that I have" (Luke 24:39 RSV)?

Jesus' resurrected body, then, was a real body, real enough to walk on the road to Emmaus, real enough to appear in the form of a gardener, real enough to eat breakfast with the disciples at Galilee. Jesus had a real body.

At the same time, this body was not a clone of his earthly body. Mark tells us that Jesus "appeared in another form" (Mark 16:12 RSV). While he was the same, he was different. So different that Mary Magdalene, his disciples on the sea, and his disciples on the path to Emmaus did not recognize him. Though he invited Thomas to touch his body, he passed through a closed door to be in Thomas's presence.

So what do we know about the resurrected body of Jesus? It was unlike any the world had ever seen.

What do we know about our resurrected bodies? They will be unlike any we have ever imagined.

Will we look so different that we aren't instantly recognized? Perhaps. (We may need nametags.) Will we be walking through walls? Chances are we'll be doing much more.

2. On a scale of one to ten (one being "terrified" and ten being "exhilarated"), how do you feel about having a heavenly body in the afterlife?

_____

_____

_____

_____

_____

_____

3. What do you think you will miss about your earthly body?

_____

_____

_____

_____

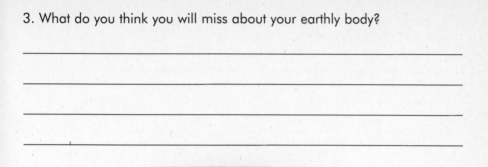

A Message from the Word

[35]But someone may ask, "How are the dead raised? What kind of body will they have?" [36]Foolish person! When you sow a seed, it must die in the ground before it can live and grow. [37]And when you sow it, it does not have the same "body" it will have later. What you sow is only a bare seed, maybe wheat or something else. [38]But God gives it a body that he has planned for it, and God gives each kind of seed its own body. [39]All things made of flesh are not the same: People have one kind of flesh, animals have another, birds have another, and fish have another. [40]Also there are heavenly bodies and earthly bodies. But the beauty of the heavenly bodies is one kind, and the beauty of the earthly bodies is another. [41]The sun has one kind of beauty, the moon has another beauty, and the stars have another. And each star is different in its beauty.

43

[42]It is the same with the dead who are raised to life. The body that is "planted" will ruin and decay, but it is raised to a life that cannot be destroyed. [43]When the body is "planted," it is without honor, but it is raised in glory. When the body is "planted," it is weak, but when it is raised, it is powerful. [44]The body that is "planted" is a physical body. When it is raised, it is a spiritual body.

There is a physical body, and there is also a spiritual body. [45]It is written in the Scriptures: "The first man, Adam, became a living person." But the last Adam became a spirit that gives life. [46]The spiritual did not come first, but the physical and then the spiritual. [47]The first man came from the dust of the earth. The second man came from heaven. [48]People who belong to the earth are like the first man of earth. But those people who belong to heaven are like the man of heaven. [49]Just as we were made like the man of earth, so we will also be made like the man of heaven.

1 Corinthians 15:35–49

4. What differences do you expect to see between our spiritual bodies and our physical bodies?

_____

_____

_____

_____

5. For what reasons do you think God gives us a body in heaven?

_____

_____

_____

_____

6. How would you describe what it might feel like to be immortal?

_____

_____

_____

More From The Word

[1]We know that our body—the tent we live in here on earth—will be destroyed. But when that happens, God will have a house for us. It will not be a house made by human hands; instead, it will be a home in heaven that will last forever. [2]But now we groan in this tent. We want God to give us our heavenly home, [3]because it will clothe us so we will not be naked. [4]While

we live in this body, we have burdens, and we groan. We do not want to be naked, but we want to be clothed with our heavenly home. Then this body that dies will be fully covered with life. ⁵This is what God made us for, and he has given us the Spirit to be a guarantee for this new life.

2 Corinthians 5:1-5

⁵⁰I tell you this, brothers and sisters: Flesh and blood cannot have a part in the kingdom of God. Something that will ruin cannot have a part in something that never ruins. ⁵¹But look! I tell you this secret: We will not all sleep in death, but we will all be changed. ⁵²It will take only a second—as quickly as an eye blinks—when the last trumpet sounds. The trumpet will sound, and those who have died will be raised to live forever, and we will all be changed. ⁵³This body that can be destroyed must clothe itself with something that can never be destroyed. And this body that dies must clothe itself with something that can never die. ⁵⁴So this body that can be destroyed will clothe itself with that which can never be destroyed, and this body that dies will clothe itself with that which can never die. When this happens, this Scripture will be made true:

"Death is destroyed forever in victory."

1 Corinthians 15:50-54

7. This passage describes our bodies as tents or houses for our souls. What other comparisons can you draw for our physical bodies?

_____

_____

_____

_____

_____

8. How does the Holy Spirit function in our lives as a deposit toward our own immortality?

_____

_____

_____

_____

9. What percentage of our time and energy do you think we spend managing our earthly bodies?

_____

_____

_____

_____

My Reflections

"Are your joints arthritic? They won't be in heaven. Is your heart weak? It will be strong in heaven. Has cancer corrupted your system? There is no cancer in heaven. Are your thoughts disjointed? Your memory failing? Your new body will have a new mind. Does this body seem closer to death than ever before? It should. It is. And unless Christ comes first, your body will be buried. Like a seed is placed in the ground, so your body will be placed in a tomb. And for a season, your soul will be in heaven while your body is in the grave. But the seed buried in the earth will blossom in heaven. Your soul and body will reunite, and you will be like Jesus." —Max

Journal

How do I see my body becoming more frail with age?

_____

_____

_____

_____

_____

For Further Study

To study more about our life in heaven, read Psalm 53:2-3; Psalm 73:25-26; Matthew 5:10-12; Matthew 6:19-21; Matthew 7:21; Luke 21:33; Philippians 3:20-21; Revelation 21:1-27.

Additional Questions

10. What about earth will you miss the least in heaven?

_____

_____

_____

_____

_____

_____

11. What is the scariest thing for you regarding death?

_____

_____

_____

_____

_____

_____

12. What emotions do you feel when you allow yourself to imagine what heaven will be like?

_____

_____

_____

_____

_____

_____

Additional Thoughts

49

_____

_____

_____

_____

_____

_____

_____

_____

_____

_____

_____

50

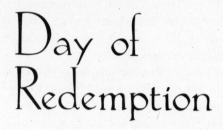

Day of Redemption

"There I am, at the entryway to heaven. My family enters, my friends enter, but when my turn comes, the door is closed. How can I know I won't be turned away?"

—Max Lucado

51

1. Why do you think most people believe they'll be allowed into heaven?

_____

_____

_____

_____

_____

_____

_____

_____

A Moment with Max

Max shares these insights with us in his book *When Christ Comes.*

Let's imagine how a person who isn't wearing the clothing of Christ appears in the eyes of heaven. For the sake of discussion, envision a decent human being...we'll call him Danny Decent. Danny, from our perspective, does everything right. He pays his taxes, pays his bills, pays attention to his family, and pays respect to his superiors. He is a good person. In fact, were we to dress him, we would dress him in white.

But heaven sees Danny differently. God sees what you and I miss. For as Mr. Decent walks through life, he makes mistakes. And every time he sins, a stain appears on his clothing. For example, he stretched the truth when he spoke to his boss yesterday. He was stained. He fudged, every so slightly, on his expense report. Another stain. From our perspective, these aren't big deals. But our perspective doesn't matter. God's does. And what God sees is a man wrapped in mistakes.

What happens if Danny changes his clothes? Suppose he goes to Christ and prays, "Lord, take away these rags. Clothe me in your grace."

If he does, here is what happens. Jesus, in an act visible only to the eyes of heaven, removes the robe of stains and replaces it with his robe of right-eousness. As a result, Danny is clothed in Christ.

God has only one requirement for entrance into heaven: that we be clothed in Christ.

52

2. Why do you think being a good person is just not good enough for God?

_____

_____

_____

_____

3. What other things (besides being clothed in Christ) does our society mistakenly assume God requires for entrance into heaven?

_____

_____

_____

_____

A Message from the Word

[26-27]You were all baptized into Christ, and so you were all clothed with Christ. This means that you are all children of God through faith in Christ Jesus. [28]In Christ, there is no difference between Jew and Greek, slave and free person, male and female. You are all the same in Christ Jesus. [29]You belong to Christ, so you are Abraham's descendants. You will inherit all of God's blessings because of the promise God made to Abraham.

[1]I want to tell you this: While those who will inherit their fathers' property are still children, they are no different from slaves. It does not matter that the children own everything. [2]While they are children, they must obey those who are chosen to care for them. But when the children reach the age set by their fathers, they are free. [3]It is the same for us. We were once like children, slaves to the useless rules of this world. [4]But when the right time came, God sent his Son who was born of a woman and lived under the law. [5]God did this so he could buy freedom for those who were under the law and so we could become his children.

[6]Since you are God's children, God sent the Spirit of his Son into your hearts, and the Spirit cries out, "Father." [7]So now you are not a slave; you are God's child, and God will give you the blessing he promised, because you are his child.

Galatians 3:26—4:7

4. Explain the difference between a slave, a son, and an heir.

_____

_____

_____

_____

5. How would you explain to someone the fact that through our faith God converts us into his own children?

_____

_____

6. Describe our inheritance as God's children.

_____

_____

_____

_____

More From The Word

²¹But God has a way to make people right with him without the law, and he has now shown us that way which the law and the prophets told us about. ²²God makes people right with himself through their faith in Jesus Christ. This is true for all who believe in Christ, because all people are the same:²³All have sinned and are not good enough for God's glory, ²⁴and all need to be made right with God by his grace, which is a free gift. They need to be made free from sin through Jesus Christ. ²⁵God gave him as a way to forgive sin through faith in the blood of Jesus' death. This showed that God always does what is right and fair, as in the past when he was patient and did not punish people for their sins. ²⁶And God gave Jesus to show today that he does what is right. God did this so he could judge rightly and so he could make right any person who has faith in Jesus.

Romans 3:21-26

7. What is the difference between a righteousness that comes through faith and a righteousness that comes through obeying the law?

_____

_____

_____

_____

_____

8. How is our righteousness like clean garments?

_____

_____

_____

_____

_____

9. How can we know if our faith here on earth is the kind that will carry us through heaven's gates?

_____

_____

_____

_____

_____

My Reflections

"Listen to how Jesus describes the inhabitants of heaven: 'They will walk with me and wear white clothes, because they are worthy.' Of all the people worthy to wear a spotless robe, Christ is. But according to the Bible he doesn't. 'He is dressed in a robe dipped in blood, and his name is the Word of God' (Revelation 19:13). Why is Christ's robe not white? Why is his cloak not spotless? Why is his garment dipped in blood? Let me answer by reminding you what Jesus did for you and me. Paul says simply, 'He changed places with us' (Galatians 3:13). He did more than remove our coat; he put on our coat. And he wore our coat of sin to the cross. As he died, his blood flowed over our sins. They were cleansed by his blood. And because of this, when Christ comes, we have no fear of being turned away at the door."

—Max

Journal

What does it mean to me that Christ has clothed me in righteousness?

_____

_____

_____

_____

_____

_____

_____

_____

_____

_____

_____

_____

_____

_____

_____

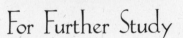

For Further Study

To study more about righteousness and salvation, read Genesis 15:6; Psalm 13:5; Psalm 35:9-10; Psalm 62:6-7; Romans 4:13-25; 2 Corinthians 7:8-10; Ephesians 4:20-24; Philippians 2:12; Hebrews 2:1-4; 1 Peter 2:23-25.

Additional Questions

10. How do you feel when you think of the sacrifice Jesus made to exchange your blood-soaked robe with his pure robe?

_____

_____

_____

_____

_____

_____

11. What is the difference between a mistake and a sin?

_____

_____

_____

_____

_____

_____

12. In what ways is becoming a Christian like changing clothes?

_____

_____

_____

_____

_____

Additional Thoughts

_____

_____

_____

_____

_____

_____

_____

_____

_____

_____

_____

_____

60

Day of Rewards

"I can understand why some will receive rewards in heaven—the martyrs, the missionaries, the heroes. But what about regular folks like me? Is there anything I can look forward to?"

—Max Lucado

61

1. Who is someone you know who you think will receive a great reward in heaven?

_____

_____

_____

_____

_____

_____

_____

_____

A Moment with Max

For all we don't know about the next life, this much is certain. The day Christ comes will be a day of reward. Those who went unknown on earth will be known in heaven. Those who never heard the cheers of men will hear the cheers of angels. Those who missed the blessing of a father will hear the blessing of their heavenly Father. The small will be great. The forgotten will be remembered. The unnoticed will be crowned and the faithful will be honored. You'll receive a crown—not just one crown, but three.

The crown of life. Can you imagine a world with no death, only life? If you can, you can imagine heaven. For citizens of heaven wear the crown of life.

What have you done today to avoid death? Likely a lot. You've popped pills, pumped pecks, passed on the pie, and pursued the polyunsaturates. Why? Because you are worried about staying alive. That won't be a worry in heaven.

The crown of righteousness. We are in a right relationship now; we are clothed with Christ. But when Jesus comes, the relationship will be made even "righter." We will be crowned with righteousness. We will be rightly related to God.

The crown of glory. Your day is coming. What the world has overlooked, your father has remembered, and sooner than you can imagine, you will be blessed by him. Look at this promise from the pen of Paul: "God will praise each one of them" (1 Corinthians 4:5).

2. Do rewards seem to be a surprising or natural part of the process of Christ's second coming? Why?

_____

_____

_____

_____

_____

3. Of the three crowns (life, righteousness, and glory), which appeals the most to you? Why?

_____

_____

_____

_____

_____

A Message from the Word

²⁷"But I say to you who are listening, love your enemies. Do good to those who hate you, ²⁸bless those who curse you, pray for those who are cruel to you. ²⁹If anyone slaps you on one cheek, offer him the other cheek, too. If someone takes your coat, do not stop him from taking your shirt. ³⁰Give to everyone who asks you, and when someone takes something that is yours, don't ask for it back. ³¹Do to others what you would want them to do to you. ³²If you love only the people who love you, what praise should you get? Even sinners love the people who love them. ³³If you do good only to those who do good to you, what praise should you get? Even sinners do that!³⁴If you lend things to people, always hoping to get something back, what praise should you get? Even sinners lend to other sinners so that they can get back the same amount!³⁵But love your enemies, do good to them, and lend to them without hoping to get anything back. Then you will have a great reward, and you will be children of the Most High God, because he is kind even to people who are ungrateful and full of sin. ³⁶Show mercy, just as your Father shows mercy."

Luke 6:27-36

63

4. In your own words, describe the kind of life that will receive a great reward.

_____

_____

_____

_____

_____

_____

5. Why do you think God will reward our faith when we owe him so much more?

_____

_____

_____

_____

6. What do you imagine heavenly rewards will consist of?

_____

_____

_____

_____

More From The Word

[1] "Be careful! When you do good things, don't do them in front of people to be seen by them. If you do that, you will have no reward from your Father in heaven.

[2] "When you give to the poor, don't be like the hypocrites. They blow trumpets in the synagogues and on the streets so that people will see them and honor them. I tell you the truth, those hypocrites already have their full reward. [3]So when you give to the poor, don't let anyone know what you are doing. [4]Your giving should be done in secret. Your Father can see what is done in secret, and he will reward you.

[5] "When you pray, don't be like the hypocrites. They love to stand in the synagogues and on the street corners and pray so people will see them. I tell you the truth, they already have their full reward. [6]When you pray, you should go into your room and close the door and pray to your Father who cannot be seen. Your Father can see what is done in secret, and he will reward you."

Matthew 6:1-6

7. What can rob us of rewards in the afterlife?

_____

_____

_____

_____

_____

8. What robs us of our spiritual rewards in this life?

_____

_____

_____

_____

65

9. How would you describe God's criteria for the rewards he has waiting for us in heaven?

_____

_____

_____

_____

_____

My Reflections

"You won't be left out. God will see to that. In fact, God himself will give the praise. When it comes to giving recognition, God does not delegate the job. God himself will praise his children. And what's more, the praise is personal!

Paul says, 'God will praise each one of them' (1 Corinthians 4:5). Awards aren't given a nation at a time, a church at a time, or a generation at a time. The crowns are given one at a time. God himself will look you in the eye and bless you. With that in mind, let me urge you to stay strong. Don't give up. Don't look back. Let Jesus speak to your heart as he says, 'Hold on to what you have, so that no one will take your crown' (Revelation 3:11 NIV)."

—Max

Journal

What things do I do that will really matter when I stand before God in heaven?

_____

_____

_____

_____

_____

_____

_____

_____

_____

_____

_____

_____

_____

67

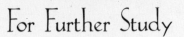

For Further Study

To study more about the rewards God promises us, read Psalm 17:14-15; Psalm 19:9-11; Proverbs 19:17; Proverbs 25:21-22; Matthew 6:1-2; Luke 6:35; Ephesians 6:8; 2 John 8-10.

Additional Questions

10. What reward would you most like to receive in heaven?

_____

_____

_____

_____

_____

_____

11. When people talk about getting "jewels" in their crowns, what do you think they mean?

_____

_____

_____

_____

_____

_____

_____

12. How do you imagine it will feel to receive a personal reward from God, the creator of the universe?

_____

_____

_____

_____

_____

_____

Additional Thoughts

_____

_____

_____

_____

_____

_____

_____

_____

_____

_____

_____

_____

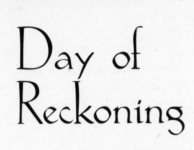

Day of Reckoning

"And what about the devil? When Christ comes, what happens to him? How do I resist him until then?" —Max Lucado

71

1. What is your concept of the devil?

_____

_____

_____

_____

_____

_____

_____

_____

A Moment with Max

Max shares these insights with us in his book *When Christ Comes.*

Suppose you had been present during the dress rehearsal of *The Wizard of Oz*. Suppose you'd seen a wide-eyed, red-headed kid hiding from the witch. And suppose you felt sorry for him. What would you have done? How would you have made him feel better?

Simple, you would have told him the rest of the story. "Sure, the witch stirs up some trouble. Yes, Dorothy and the guys have their problems. But in the end, the witch melts like wax and everyone gets home safely."

Isn't that what God has told us about Satan? Read again the words of John: "The Devil who deceived them [God's people] will be hurled into Lake Fire and Brimstone, joining the Beast and False prophet, the three in torment around the clock for ages without end" (Revelation 20:10 MSG).

God has kept no secrets. He has told us that, while on this yellow brick road, we will experience trouble. Disease will afflict bodies. Divorce will break hearts. Death will make widows, and devastation will destroy countries. We should not expect any less. But just because the devil shows up and cackles, we needn't panic.

It is finished. The battle is over. Be alert. But don't be alarmed. The witch has no power. The manuscript has been published. The book has been bound. Satan is loosed for a season, but the season is oh-so-brief. Just a few more scenes, just a few more turns in the road, and his end will come.

2. In what ways can you compare Satan to the witch in *The Wizard of Oz*?

_____

_____

_____

_____

3. How would you compare your life's journey to Dorothy's on the yellow brick road?

_____

_____

_____

_____

A Message from the Word

¹I saw an angel coming down from heaven. He had the key to the bottomless pit and a large chain in his hand. ²The angel grabbed the dragon, that old snake who is the devil and Satan, and tied him up for a thousand years. ³Then he threw him into the bottomless pit, closed it, and locked it over him. The angel did this so he could not trick the people of the earth anymore until the thousand years were ended. After a thousand years he must be set free for a short time.

⁴Then I saw some thrones and people sitting on them who had been given the power to judge. And I saw the souls of those who had been killed because they were faithful to the message of Jesus and the message from God. They had not worshiped the beast or his idol, and they had not received the mark of the beast on their foreheads or on their hands. They came back to life and ruled with Christ for a thousand years. ⁵ (The others that were dead did not live again until the thousand years were ended.) This is the first raising of the dead. ⁶Happy and holy are those who share in this first raising of the dead. The second death has no power over them. They will be priests for God and for Christ and will rule with him for a thousand years.

⁷When the thousand years are over, Satan will be set free from his prison. ⁸Then he will go out to trick the nations in all the earth—Gog and Magog—to gather them for battle. There are so many people they will be like sand on the seashore. ⁹And Satan's army marched across the earth and gathered around the camp of God's people and the city God loves. But fire came down from heaven and burned them up. ¹⁰And Satan, who tricked them, was thrown into the lake of burning sulfur with the beast and the false prophet. There they will be punished day and night forever and ever.

Revelation 20:1-10

73

4. What do you think is Satan's motivation for trying to destroy God's plans, even though his end is inevitable?

_____

_____

_____

_____

5. List some of Satan's greatest acts of destruction that you see around you today.

_____

_____

_____

_____

_____

6. How can you face life differently knowing that there is a closing chapter for Satan's power and reign?

_____

_____

_____

_____

_____

More From The Word

[7]Then there was a war in heaven. Michael and his angels fought against the dragon, and the dragon and his angels fought back. [8]But the dragon was not strong enough, and he and his angels lost their place in heaven. [9]The giant dragon was thrown down out of heaven. (He is that old snake called the devil or Satan, who tricks the whole world.) The dragon with his angels was thrown down to the earth.
[10]Then I heard a loud voice in heaven saying:
"The salvation and the power and the kingdom of our God
    and the authority of his Christ have now come.
The accuser of our brothers and sisters,
    who accused them day and night before our God,

has been thrown down.
¹¹And our brothers and sisters defeated him
   by the blood of the Lamb's death
   and by the message they preached.
They did not love their lives so much
   that they were afraid of death.
¹²So rejoice, you heavens
   and all who live there!
But it will be terrible for the earth and the sea,
   because the devil has come down to you!
He is filled with anger,
   because he knows he does not have much time."

Revelation 12:7–12

7. Why do you suppose Satan continues to rebel against God rather than repent?

_____

_____

_____ 75

_____

8. How do you imagine the battle of Armageddon?

_____

_____

_____

_____

9. How would you compare the power of God to the power of Satan?

_____

_____

_____

_____

My Reflections

"The presence of Satan is one reason some people fear the return of Christ. Understandably so. Terms such as 'Armageddon,' 'lake of fire,' and the 'scarlet beast' are enough to unnerve the stoutest heart. And certainly those who do not know God have reason to be anxious. But those dressed in Christ? No. They need only read the manuscript's final reference to the devil. 'Satan, who tricked them [God's people], was thrown into the lake of burning sulfur with the beast and the false prophet. There they will be punished day and night forever and ever' (Revelation 20:10). God hasn't kept the ending a secret. He wants us to see the big picture. He wants us to know that he wins. And he also wants us to know that the evil we witness on the stage of life is not as mighty as we might think." —Max

Journal

In what areas do I need more help in resisting the devil?

_____

_____

_____

_____

_____

_____

_____

_____

_____

_____

77

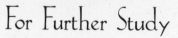

For Further Study

To study more about Satan, read 1 Chronicles 21:1; Job 1:6–12; Matthew 4:1–11; Matthew 8:28–31; Luke 22:3–6; 2 Corinthians 2:10–11; Hebrews 2:14–15; Revelation 12:9; Revelation 20:10.

Additional Questions

10. What do you think is the most harmful stereotype we have of the devil?

_____

_____

_____

_____

_____

_____

11. What do you think is the most helpful stereotype we have of the devil?

_____

_____

_____

_____

_____

_____

12. If you could ask Satan one question (and get an honest answer), what would it be?

_____

_____

_____

_____

_____

_____

Additional Thoughts

_____

_____

_____

_____

_____

_____

_____

_____

_____

Day of Permanent Pardon

"The thought of judgment day troubles me. Everything I've ever done will be revealed, right? But why is that necessary? And when all my secret sins are made public, won't I be ashamed? Humiliated?" —Max Lucado

81

1. What kinds of sins do you think people would be most concerned with having revealed on judgment day?

_____

_____

_____

_____

_____

_____

_____

A Moment with Max

The day Christ comes will be a day of judgment. This judgment will be marked by three accomplishments.

First, God's grace will be revealed. Our host will receive all the credit and attention.

Second, rewards for his servants will be unveiled. Those who accepted his invitation will be uniquely honored.

And third, those who do not know him will pay a price. A severe, terrible price.

Jesus summarizes the matter in Luke 12:2: "Everything that is hidden will be shown, and everything that is secret will be made known."

Even for the believer? Will we be judged as well? If we are clothed in Christ, why do we need a judgment at all?

Is Jesus saying that all secrets will be revealed? The secrets of sinners and saints alike? He is, but—and this is essential—the sins of the saved will be revealed as *forgiven* sins. Our transgressions will be announced as *pardoned* transgressions. That is the second reason believers will be judged. The first, so our acts can be rewarded and second, so that God's grace can be revealed.

82

2. When you think of your life being revealed before everyone in the world, how do you feel?

_____

_____

_____

_____

3. Why do you think we fear public judgment so much when God sees what we do every moment that we live?

_____

_____

_____

_____

A Message from the Word

[11]Then I saw a great white throne and the One who was sitting on it. Earth and sky ran away from him and disappeared. [12]And I saw the dead, great and small, standing before the throne. Then books were opened, and the book of life was opened. The dead were judged by what they had done, which was written in the books. [13]The sea gave up the dead who were in it, and Death and Hades gave up the dead who were in them. Each person was judged by what he had done. [14]And Death and Hades were thrown into the lake of fire. The lake of fire is the second death. [15]And anyone whose name was not found written in the book of life was thrown into the lake of fire.

[1]Then I saw a new heaven and a new earth. The first heaven and the first earth had disappeared, and there was no sea anymore. [2]And I saw the holy city, the new Jerusalem, coming down out of heaven from God. It was prepared like a bride dressed for her husband. [3]And I heard a loud voice from the throne, saying, "Now God's presence is with people, and he will live with them, and they will be his people. God himself will be with them and will be their God. [4]He will wipe away every tear from their eyes, and there will be no more death, sadness, crying, or pain, because all the old ways are gone."

[5]The One who was sitting on the throne said, "Look! I am making everything new!" Then he said, "Write this, because these words are true and can be trusted."

Revelation 20:11—21:5

4. What words come to mind when you imagine standing before a huge throne with God, as Judge, sitting on it?

_____

_____

_____

_____

_____

5. How do you imagine the new heaven and earth?

_____

_____

_____

_____

_____

6. What are some of the negative things of this world that will pass away?

_____

_____

_____

_____

_____

More From The Word

[31]"The Son of Man will come again in his great glory, with all his angels. He will be King and sit on his great throne. [32]All the nations of the world will be gathered before him, and he will separate them into two groups as a shepherd separates the sheep from the goats. [33]The Son of Man will put the sheep on his right and the goats on his left.

[34]"Then the King will say to the people on his right, 'Come, my Father has given you his blessing. Receive the kingdom God has prepared for you since the world was made. [35]I was hungry, and you gave me food. I was thirsty, and you gave me something to drink. I was alone and away from home, and you invited me into your house. [36]I was without clothes, and you gave me something to wear. I was sick, and you cared for me. I was in prison, and you visited me.'

[37]"Then the good people will answer, 'Lord, when did we see you hungry

and give you food, or thirsty and give you something to drink?[38]When did we see you alone and away from home and invite you into our house? When did we see you without clothes and give you something to wear?[39]When did we see you sick or in prison and care for you?'

[40]"Then the King will answer, 'I tell you the truth, anything you did for even the least of my people here, you also did for me.'"

Matthew 25:31-40

7. Explain how helping our fellowman translates to helping God.

_____

_____

_____

_____

_____

8. According to this passage, what do you think is the difference between a sheep and a goat?

_____

_____

_____

_____

9. If our greatest concern during the judgment will not be what everyone else is thinking of us, what do you think it will be?

_____

_____

_____

_____

_____

My Reflections

"Perhaps you're thinking, *It will be triumph for him, but humiliation for me.* No, it won't. Scripture promises, 'The one who trusts in him will never be put to shame' (1 Peter 2:6 NIV). But how can this be; won't I be embarrassed beyond recovery? No, you won't. Here is why. Shame is a child of self-centeredness. Heaven's occupants are not self-centered, they are Christ-centered. You will be in your sinless state. The sinless don't protect a reputation or protect an image. You won't be ashamed. You'll be happy to let God do in heaven what he did on earth—be honored in your weaknesses. Heads bowed in shame? No. Heads bowed in worship? No doubt." —Max

Journal

In what circumstances is it most difficult for me to rest in God's grace?

_____

_____

_____

_____

_____

_____

_____

_____

_____

_____

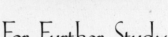

For Further Study

To study more about God's judgment, read 1 Samuel 2:10; Romans 14:9-13; 1 Corinthians 11:27-34; Hebrews 4:12; 1 Peter 1:17; 1 Peter 4:17; 2 Peter 2:4-10; Revelation 6:9-11; Revelation 14:6-7; Revelation 19:11-15.

Additional Questions

10. What visual image do you get when you think of the final judgment?

_____

_____

_____

_____

_____

_____

11. Why do you think God wants to review all our lives?

_____

_____

_____

_____

_____

_____

_____

12. In what ways does the promise of judgment keep us out of trouble?

_____

_____

_____

_____

_____

_____

Additional Thoughts

_____

_____

_____

_____

_____

_____

_____

_____

_____

_____

_____

_____

_____

Day of Ultimate Justice

"My question has to do with hell. Does it exist? If so, why? Why would a loving God send people to hell?" —*Max Lucado*

1. What images of hell have you seen depicted by artists or the media? How did those images make you feel?

_____

_____

_____

_____

_____

_____

_____

A Moment with Max

Max shares these insights with us in his book *When Christ Comes*.

If there is no hell, God is not just. If there is no punishment of sin, heaven is apathetic toward the rapists and pillagers and mass murderers of society. If there is no hell, God is blind toward the victims and has turned his back on those who pray for relief. If there is no wrath toward evil, then God is not love, for love hates that which is evil.

To say there is no hell is also to say God is a liar and his Scripture untrue.

God does not *send* people to hell. He simply honors their choice. Hell is the ultimate expression of God's high regard for the dignity of man. He has never forced us to choose him, even when that means we would choose hell. As C.S. Lewis stated: "There are only two kinds of people in the end: those who say to God, 'Thy will be done' and those to whom God says, in the end, 'thy will be done.' All that are in hell choose it."

No, God does not "send" people to hell. Nor does he send "people" to hell. That is the second misconception.

The word *people* is neutral, implying innocence. Nowhere does Scripture teach that innocent people are condemned. People do not go to hell. Sinners do. The rebellious do. The self-centered do. So how could a loving God send people to hell? He doesn't. He simply honors the choice of sinners.

92

2. Why do you think, given the choice, some would choose hell?

_____

_____

_____

_____

3. What do you think will be the most miserable thing about hell?

_____

_____

_____

_____

A Message from the Word

⁴When angels sinned, God did not let them go free without punishment. He sent them to hell and put them in caves of darkness where they are being held for judgment. ⁵And God punished the world long ago when he brought a flood to the world that was full of people who were against him. But God saved Noah, who preached about being right with God, and seven other people with him. ⁶And God also destroyed the evil cities of Sodom and Gomorrah by burning them until they were ashes. He made those cities an example of what will happen to those who are against God. ⁷But he saved Lot from those cities. Lot, a good man, was troubled because of the filthy lives of evil people. ⁸ (Lot was a good man, but because he lived with evil people every day, his good heart was hurt by the evil things he saw and heard.)⁹So the Lord knows how to save those who serve him when troubles come. He will hold evil people and punish them, while waiting for the Judgment Day. ¹⁰That punishment is especially for those who live by doing the evil things their sinful selves want and who hate authority.

These false teachers are bold and do anything they want. They are not afraid to speak against the angels. ¹¹But even the angels, who are much stronger and more powerful than false teachers, do not accuse them with insults before the Lord. ¹²But these people speak against things they do not understand. They are like animals that act without thinking, animals born to be caught and killed. And, like animals, these false teachers will be destroyed. ¹³They have caused many people to suffer, so they themselves will suffer. That is their pay for what they have done. They take pleasure in openly doing evil, so they are like dirty spots and stains among you. They delight in trickery while eating meals with you. ¹⁴Every time they look at a woman they want her, and their desire for sin is never satisfied. They lead weak people into the trap of sin, and they have taught their hearts to be greedy. God will punish them!

2 Peter 2:4-14

4. According to this passage, what kinds of people will end up in hell?

_____

_____

_____

_____

5. Why is the reality of hell so difficult for us to reconcile with a loving God?

_____

_____

_____

_____

6. Why do you think God revealed to us the existence of a place like hell?

_____

_____

_____

_____

More From The Word

[26]"So don't be afraid of those people, because everything that is hidden will be shown. Everything that is secret will be made known. [27]I tell you these things in the dark, but I want you to tell them in the light. What you hear whispered in your ear you should shout from the housetops. [28]Don't be afraid of people, who can kill the body but cannot kill the soul. The only one you should fear is the one who can destroy the soul and the body in hell. [29]Two sparrows cost only a penny, but not even one of them can die without your Father's knowing it. [30]God even knows how many hairs are on your head. [31]So don't be afraid. You are worth much more than many sparrows.

[32]"All those who stand before others and say they believe in me, I will say before my Father in heaven that they belong to me. [33]But all who stand before others and say they do not believe in me, I will say before my Father in heaven that they do not belong to me."

Matthew 10:26-33

7. In what ways can we acknowledge Jesus before men?

_____

_____

_____

_____

_____

8. Why do we often bow to men's approval more than God's even though he is the one with the power over our soul's destiny?

_____

_____

_____

_____

9. What is the simplest explanation you can give someone for how to avoid hell?

_____

_____

_____

_____

_____

My Reflections

"Yes, hell's misery is deep, but not as deep as God's love. So how do we apply this message? If you are saved, it should cause you to rejoice. You've been rescued. A glance into hell leads the believer to rejoice. But it also leads the believer to redouble his efforts to reach the lost. To understand hell is to pray more earnestly and to serve more diligently. Ours is a high-stakes mission. And the lost? What is the meaning of this message for the unprepared? Heed the warnings and get ready. This plane won't fly forever. 'Death is the destiny of every man; the living should take this to heart' (Ecclesiastes 7:2 NIV)." —Max

Journal

What does the existence of hell mean for me?

_____

_____

_____

_____

_____

_____

_____

_____

_____

_____

_____

_____

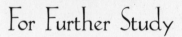

For Further Study

To study more about hell, read Matthew 5:29-30; Matthew 10:28; Matthew 16:18; Matthew 18:9; Luke 16:19-28; Revelation 1:17-18.

Additional Questions

10. Where did you first hear about hell?

11. What do you most fear about hell?

12. How does the reality of hell motivate you to evangelize your friends and family members?

_____

_____

_____

_____

_____

_____

Additional Thoughts

_____

_____

_____

_____

_____

_____

_____

_____

_____

_____

_____

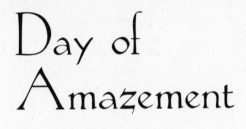

Day of Amazement

"Will everyone see Jesus? And forgive me for asking, would I want to? No sight is beautiful forever. What makes Jesus the exception?"
—Max Lucado

1. What do you imagine it will be like to see Jesus for the first time?

_____

_____

_____

_____

_____

_____

_____

_____

A Moment with Max

Max shares these insights with us in his book *When Christ Comes*.

"No disrespect intended. Of course I want to see Jesus. But to see him *forever!?* Will he be that amazing?"

According to Paul he will. "On the day when the Lord Jesus comes," he writes, "all people who have believed will be amazed at Jesus" (2 Thessalonians 1:10).

Amazed at Jesus. Not amazed at angels or mansions or new bodies or new creations. Paul doesn't measure the joy of encountering the apostles or embracing our loved ones. If we will be amazed at these, which certainly we will, he does not say. What he does say is that we will be amazed at Jesus.

What we have only seen in our thoughts, we will see with our eyes. What we've struggled to imagine, we will be free to behold. What we've seen in a glimpse, we will then see in full view. And, according to Paul, we will be amazed.

What will be so amazing?

Of course I have no way of answering that question from personal experience. But I can lead you to someone who can. One Sunday morning many Sundays ago, a man named John saw Jesus. And what he saw, he recorded, and what he recorded has tantalized seekers of Christ for two thousand years.

102

2. Describe someone you know who longs to see Christ.

_____

_____

_____

_____

3. What will make us long to see Christ when we get to heaven?

_____

_____

_____

_____

A Message from the Word

²²Who is the liar? It is the person who does not accept Jesus as the Christ. This is the enemy of Christ: the person who does not accept the Father and his Son. ²³Whoever does not accept the Son does not have the Father. But whoever confesses the Son has the Father, too.

²⁴Be sure you continue to follow the teaching you heard from the beginning. If you continue to follow what you heard from the beginning, you will stay in the Son and in the Father. ²⁵And this is what the Son promised to us—life forever.

²⁶I am writing this letter about those people who are trying to lead you the wrong way. ²⁷Christ gave you a special gift that is still in you, so you do not need any other teacher. His gift teaches you about everything, and it is true, not false. So continue to live in Christ, as his gift taught you.

²⁸Yes, my dear children, live in him so that when Christ comes back, we can be without fear and not be ashamed in his presence. ²⁹If you know that Christ is all that is right, you know that all who do right are God's children.

¹The Father has loved us so much that we are called children of God. And we really are his children. The reason the people in the world do not know us is that they have not known him. ²Dear friends, now we are children of God, and we have not yet been shown what we will be in the future. But we know that when Christ comes again, we will be like him, because we will see him as he really is. ³Christ is pure, and all who have this hope in Christ keep themselves pure like Christ.

1 John 2:22—3:3

4. How do you explain the fact that seeing Christ will bring about such changes in us?

_____

_____

_____

_____

_____

_____

5. In what ways does seeing Christ's purity make us more pure?

_____

_____

_____

_____

_____

6. How does the anticipation of seeing Jesus face to face change the way you want to live your life?

_____

_____

_____

_____

More From The Word

¹²I turned to see who was talking to me. When I turned, I saw seven golden lampstands ¹³and someone among the lampstands who was "like a Son of Man." He was dressed in a long robe and had a gold band around his chest. ¹⁴His head and hair were white like wool, as white as snow, and his eyes were like flames of fire. ¹⁵His feet were like bronze that glows hot in a furnace, and his voice was like the noise of flooding water. ¹⁶He held seven stars in his right hand, and a sharp double-edged sword came out of his mouth. He looked like the sun shining at its brightest time.

¹⁷When I saw him, I fell down at his feet like a dead man. He put his right hand on me and said, "Do not be afraid. I am the First and the Last. ¹⁸I am the One who lives; I was dead, but look, I am alive forever and ever! And I hold the keys to death and to the place of the dead.

Revelation 1:12–18

7. What does it mean for you that Christ holds the keys of death and hell?

_____

_____

_____

_____

_____

8. Which of the images described in this passage stands out the most to you? Why?

_____

_____

_____

_____

_____

9. What attributes of this life keep us from seeing Jesus now as he really is?

_____

_____

_____

_____

_____

My Reflections

"What will happen when you see Jesus? You will see unblemished purity and unending strength. You will feel his unending presence and know his unbridled protection. And all that he is, you will be, for you will be like Jesus.

Wasn't that the promise of John? 'We know that when Christ comes again, we will be like him, because we will see him as he really is' (1 John 3:2). Since you'll be pure as snow, you will never sin again. Since you'll be as strong as bronze, you will never stumble again. Since you'll dwell near the river, you will never feel lonely again. Since the work of the priest will have been finished, you will never doubt again. When Christ comes, you will dwell in the light of God. And you will see him as he really is." —Max

Journal

What will be changed the most about me when I become like Jesus?

_____

_____

_____

_____

_____

_____

_____

_____

_____

_____

_____

_____

For Further Study

To study more about how Jesus changes us, read Romans 8:28-30;
Philippians 3:7-11;1 John 3:2.

Additional Questions

10. If you could make it happen, what would your first conversation with
Jesus be about?

_____

_____

_____

_____

_____

_____

11. How can looking forward to heaven change our perspective on
earth?

_____

_____

_____

_____

_____

_____

12. Describe how you think society will function in the new heaven and earth.

_____

_____

_____

_____

_____

_____

Additional Thoughts

_____

_____

_____

_____

_____

_____

_____

_____

_____

_____

_____

_____

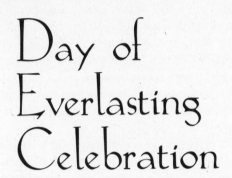

Day of Everlasting Celebration

"Why would Jesus come for me? Compared to others, I'm so ordinary. And I've made so many mistakes. Why would he be interested in me?"
—*Max Lucado*

1. If someone asked you why Jesus would come back to earth for you, how would you respond?

_____

_____

_____

_____

_____

_____

_____

_____

A Moment with Max

Look long enough in the eyes of our Savior and, there you will see a bride....He sees her, he awaits her, he longs for her.

And who is that bride? Who is this beauty who occupies the heart of Jesus?

You are. You have captured the heart of God. "As a man rejoices over his new wife, so your God will rejoice over you" (Isaiah 62:5).

The challenge is to remember that. To meditate on it. To focus on it. To allow his love to change the way you look at you.

You have been chosen by Christ. You are released from your old life in your old house, and he has claimed you as his beloved. "Then where is he?" you might ask. "Why hasn't he come?"

There is only one answer. His bride is not ready. She is still being prepared.

Engaged people are obsessed with preparation. The right dress. The right weight. The right hair and the right tux. They want everything to be right. Why? So their fiancé will marry them? No. Just the opposite. They want to look their best *because* their fiancé is marrying them.

The same is true for us. We want to look our best for Christ. We want our hearts to be pure and our thoughts to be clean. We want our faces to shine with grace and our eyes to sparkle with love. We want to be prepared.

Why? In hopes that he will love us? No. Just the opposite, because he already does.

2. What keeps us from believing that God longs to be with us?

_____

_____

_____

_____

3. In what ways does the church in today's society need to be more prepared to meet her groom, Christ?

_____

_____

_____

_____

A Message from the Word

¹ "At that time the kingdom of heaven will be like ten bridesmaids who took their lamps and went to wait for the bridegroom. ²Five of them were foolish and five were wise. ³The five foolish bridesmaids took their lamps, but they did not take more oil for the lamps to burn. ⁴The wise bridesmaids took their lamps and more oil in jars. ⁵Because the bridegroom was late, they became sleepy and went to sleep.

⁶ "At midnight someone cried out, 'The bridegroom is coming! Come and meet him!' ⁷Then all the bridesmaids woke up and got their lamps ready. ⁸But the foolish ones said to the wise, 'Give us some of your oil, because our lamps are going out.' ⁹The wise bridesmaids answered, 'No, the oil we have might not be enough for all of us. Go to the people who sell oil and buy some for yourselves.'

¹⁰ "So while the five foolish bridesmaids went to buy oil, the bridegroom came. The bridesmaids who were ready went in with the bridegroom to the wedding feast. Then the door was closed and locked.

¹¹ "Later the others came back and said, 'Sir, sir, open the door to let us in.' ¹²But the bridegroom answered, 'I tell you the truth, I don't want to know you.'

¹³ "So always be ready, because you don't know the day or the hour the Son of Man will come."

Matthew 25:1-13

4. What kind of life do we need to live to be ready for Jesus, our spiritual bridegroom?

_____

_____

_____

_____

_____

_____

5. What elements of our lives could represent the oil in the virgins' lamps?

_____

_____

_____

_____

_____

6. For what reasons do you think God chose to keep the time of Christ's return a secret?

_____

_____

_____

_____

_____

_____

More From The Word

[36]"No one knows when that day or time will be, not the angels in heaven, not even the Son. Only the Father knows. [37]When the Son of Man comes, it will be like what happened during Noah's time. [38]In those days before the flood, people were eating and drinking, marrying and giving their children to be married, until the day Noah entered the boat. [39]They knew nothing about what was happening until the flood came and destroyed them. It will be the same when the Son of Man comes. [40]Two men will be in the field. One will be taken, and the other will be left. [41]Two women will be grinding grain with a mill. One will be taken, and the other will be left.

⁴²"So always be ready, because you don't know the day your Lord will come. ⁴³Remember this: If the owner of the house knew what time of night a thief was coming, the owner would watch and not let the thief break in. ⁴⁴So you also must be ready, because the Son of Man will come at a time you don't expect him."

Matthew 24:36-44

7. Does the unexpected nature of Christ's return make you more wary or less wary about his coming?

_____

_____

_____

_____

_____

8. What kinds of things give us confidence and comfort as we wait for Christ's coming?

_____

_____

_____

_____

9. Describe the ways that we can keep watch for Christ's return, even though the timing will be unexpected.

_____

_____

_____

_____

_____

My Reflections

"You are spoken for. You are engaged, set apart, called out, a holy bride. Forbidden waters hold nothing for you. You have been chosen for his castle. Don't settle for one-night stands in the arms of a stranger. Be obsessed with your wedding date. Guard against forgetfulness. Be intolerant of memory lapses. Write yourself notes. Memorize verses. Do whatever you need to do to remember. 'Aim at what is in heaven…Think only about the things in heaven' (Colossians 3:1-2). You are engaged to royalty, and your Prince is coming to take you home." —Max

Journal

If I'm the bride of Christ, what distracts me from my wedding day?

_____

_____

_____

_____

_____

_____

_____

_____

_____

_____

For Further Study

To study more about the bride of Christ, read Mark 2:18-20; John 3:27-30; Ephesians 5:25-28; Revelation 19:6-9; Revelation 22:17.

Additional Questions

10. List some comparisons between a married couple and Jesus and his church.

_____

_____

_____

_____

_____

_____

_____

11. What do you think will be the greatest benefit of being Christ's bride?

_____

_____

_____

_____

_____

_____

_____

12. In what ways do you think we can best prepare for seeing Jesus?

_____

_____

_____

_____

_____

_____

_____

Additional Thoughts

_____

_____

_____

_____

_____

_____

_____

_____

_____

_____

120